Winter
Here and There

By Charnan Simon

Winter is not the same in all places. Read about different winters. Think about the kind of winter you like.

PEARSON

Winter is different from other **seasons**. It is colder than spring, summer, or fall. But winter is not the same everywhere in our country.

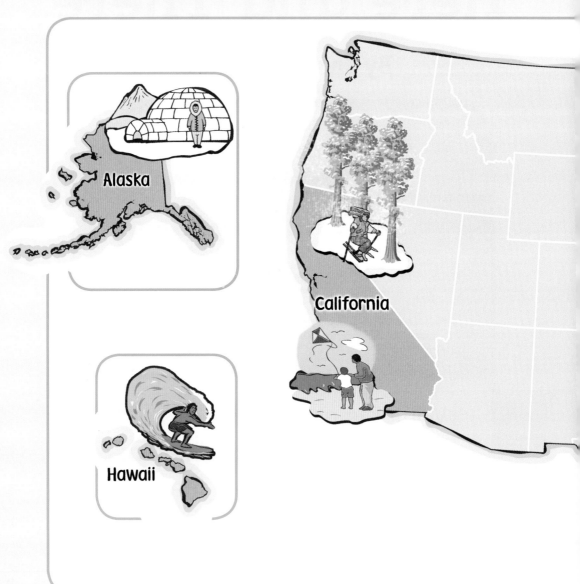

Alaska

California

Hawaii

Winter is a very cold **season** in some places. In other places, it is not very cold at all.

Vermont

United States

Florida

Winter in Vermont can be very cold. People wear coats, hats, and **mittens** when they go outside. Sometimes a lot of snow falls and icy winds blow.

People play outside in the snow. Coats, hats, and **mittens** keep them warm.

Animals also need to stay warm in winter. Some animals find warm places to live. They might live in holes in trees or underground. Other animals grow thick fur to keep warm.

White fur helps animals to hide in the snow.

Other animals spend the winter sleeping. They find warm places where they are safe.

The chipmunk will sleep until spring.

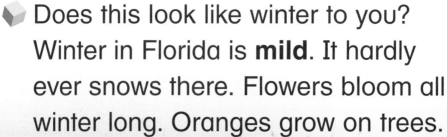 Does this look like winter to you? Winter in Florida is **mild**. It hardly ever snows there. Flowers bloom all winter long. Oranges grow on trees.

The air is **mild**. The sun is warm.
Children can play outside all day.

Many people visit Florida in the winter. They go to swim in the ocean. They go to enjoy the warm and sunny days. They go to get away from cold winters in other places.

Many birds go to Florida in the winter. They go to stay warm and to find food. Then they fly away in the spring.

This bird spends the winter in Florida.

Winter on the **coast** of California is not very cold. It rains, but it almost never snows. People can fly kites and play sports on the beach. But winter in the mountains is different.

It rains a lot on the **coast**. But in the mountains, it snows a lot. People have fun doing winter sports.

Winter is a special season. It can be mild or cold. It can bring rain or snow. Winter means different things in different places.

It is warm in most parts of Hawaii—even on winter days.

Winter is different here and there!
Winter is special everywhere!

Winter in Alaska is snowy and very cold.

Glossary

coast land along the ocean

mild warm; not hot or cold

mittens warm covers for the hands

seasons the four times of the year: spring, summer, fall, and winter